UNCOVERING PATHWAYS TOWARDS AN INCLUSIVE GREEN ECONOMY

A SUMMARY FOR LEADERS

UNCOVERING
PATHWAYS
TOWARDS AN
INCLUSIVE
GREEN ECONOMY

A SUMMARY FOR
LEADERS

Director of Publication:
Naysán Sabha

Lead authors:
Sheng Fulai, Isabell Kempf, Pushpam Kumar, Ligia Noronha, Steven Stone and Pavan Sukhdev.

Coordination:
Angeline Djampou

Design & Layout:
William Orlale

* All dollar ($) amounts refer to US dollars.

Contents

UNCOVERING
PATHWAYS
TOWARDS AN
INCLUSIVE
GREEN ECONOMY

A SUMMARY FOR
LEADERS

❭ CONTENTS

Message from Achim Steiner

B

UNCOVERING
PATHWAYS
TOWARDS AN
INCLUSIVE
GREEN ECONOMY

A SUMMARY FOR
LEADERS

❯ MESSAGE
FROM ACHIM
STEINER

We live in a world of imminent ecological thresholds and environmental tipping points, continuing social disparities and persistent poverty. Emerging global threats to "Our Common Future" require much greater collective action, improved benefit sharing from natural resource development and greater financing to enable transformative action. And driving this change we need a new moral imperative linked to equitable outcomes, shared concerns, and equal claims, including the rights of future generations. We need to evolve to a new economic model, capable of progressing and achieving the goals of sustainable development, and one that matches the ambition of countries as they embark on implementing the 2030 Agenda for Sustainable Development.

An **Inclusive Green Economy** (IGE) has evolved from earlier work on Green Economy. In its simplest expression, such an economy is low carbon, efficient and clean in production, but also inclusive in consumption and outcomes, based on sharing, circularity, collaboration, solidarity, resilience, opportunity, and interdependence. It is focused on expanding options and choices for national economies, using targeted and appropriate fiscal and social protection policies, and backed up by strong institutions that are specifically geared to safeguarding social and ecological floors. And it recognizes that there are many and diverse pathways to environmental sustainability.

This paper speaks to the multiple benefits – economic, health, security, social and environmental – that such an approach can bring to nations, mindful of the differing challenges faced by states along the development continuum, be they developed, developing, emerging, or in conflict. It argues for policies that are nuanced, context-dependent, and modulated. An integrated approach can help states understand how to maximize, prioritize, and sequence the different benefits to human well-being that can be derived from a healthy environment.

At the end of the day, an inclusive green economy must provide not only for jobs and income, but for our health, our environment and our future. This is our common challenge: creating the conditions for enhanced prosperity and growing social equity, within the contours of a finite and fragile planet.

Achim Steiner
United Nations Under-Secretary-General and
Executive Director, United Nations Environment Programme

Acknowledgements

This paper has benefited from the contributions of a wide array of individuals as it evolved from an early concept to the document you now have before you.

Initial thinking was catalyzed by a brainstorming retreat in Abu Dhabi on the role for UNEP in a *"post-Rio+20"* world with UNEP Senior Managers and key partners. This retreat was followed by an intense series of reflections and conversations facilitated by Mark Halle and a team at the International Institute for Sustainable Development, who were engaged to support UNEP in envisioning the broad contours of a *"Green Economy 2.0."* We are grateful to Mark and colleagues for their support and creative energy and enthusiasm, constantly raising the bar in terms of ambition and keeping our eyes on the horizon.

A broad and inclusive team from UNEP then took the baton forward, composed of a core authoring group including Sheng Fulai, Isabell Kempf, Pushpam Kumar, Ligia Noronha, and Steven Stone. This core group was ably supported by a much larger set of contributors from across UNEP, including, Iyad Abumoghli, Jacqueline Alder (now with FAO), Charles Arden-Clarke, Wondwosen Asnake, Margarita Astralaga (now with IFAD), Dolores Barrientos, Matthew Billot, Christophe Bouvier, Noah Bucon, Michele Candotti, Sara Castro, Munyaradzi Chenje, Tim Christophersen, Matias Gallardo, Dorothee Georg, Julie Godin, Elliot Harris, Arab Hoballah, Salman Hussain, David Jensen, Tim Kasten, Jorge Lacuna Celis, Shaoyi Li, Eirik Lindebjerg (now with WWF), Daiana Marino, Jacqueline McGlade, Anja von Moltke, Chiara Moroni, Elizabeth Mrema, Mara Murillo, Asad Naqvi, Maryam Niamir-Fuller, Martina Otto, Alberto Pacheco, Rowan Palmer, Pierre Quiblier, Mark Radka, James Rawles, Nick Robins, Benjamin Simmons, Elisa Tonda, Robert Wabunoha, Vera Weick, Mette Wilke, Wanhua Yang, Adriana Zacarias, Simon Zadek, Victoria Luque and Kaveh Zahedi. We would like to thank each and every person for their insights and contributions to this collective endeavor.

The guidance and support of Achim Steiner, the Executive Director and Ibrahim Thiaw, the Deputy Executive Director of UNEP were invaluable throughout the process. Finally, and importantly, we are particularly grateful to Pavan Sukhdev, Chief Executive Officer of GIST Advisory & UNEP Goodwill Ambassador, for his thorough external review and direct engagement with drafting the short version of this paper, which you now have in your hands.

Any remaining errors and omissions are the responsibility of the core authoring team.

UNCOVERING
PATHWAYS
TOWARDS AN
INCLUSIVE
GREEN ECONOMY

A SUMMARY FOR
LEADERS

> **ACKNOWLEDGEMENTS**

1

**UNCOVERING
PATHWAYS
TOWARDS AN
INCLUSIVE
GREEN ECONOMY**

A SUMMARY FOR
LEADERS

> VISIONING
TOMORROW

"Visioning an economy fit for our future." © BLUECARBON

Visioning Tomorrow

1

UNCOVERING
PATHWAYS
TOWARDS AN
INCLUSIVE
GREEN ECONOMY

A SUMMARY FOR
LEADERS

❯ VISIONING
TOMORROW

AN ECONOMY OF PERMANENCE

In his essay "The Economics of the Coming Spaceship Earth"[1] (1966), Ken Boulding used an apt phrase to describe the economy of his time: *"cowboy economy."* In this economy, he wrote, success was measured by the amount of throughput from factors of production (labor, land, and capital), and there were infinite reservoirs for extracting raw materials and receiving waste. Boulding went on to describe an alternative that he deemed much more appropriate for human survival and success: the *"spaceman economy,"* where throughput would be something to be minimized and the measure of success would not be in production or consumption but in the nature, extent, quality, and complexity of total capital stock available to humans, including the state of human bodies and minds.

Unfortunately, half a century later, our dominant economic model still remains Boulding's 'cowboy economy'. However, we are now much better positioned to understand and measure its hidden costs and predict their consequences. We now have the science, technology, social and economic analysis we need to design transitions towards more sustainable and equitable models. The "Inclusive Green Economy" we describe here is one such model.

The quest for 'sustainability' - of a society or of an economy - is in essence a quest for permanence. Nature, with all its diverse, abundant and cyclical rhythms of life, best typifies the kind of 'permanence' that has eluded human civilizations ever since *homo sapiens* learnt to mould their environments to meet their needs. J.C.Kumarappa, an economist collaborator of Mahatma Gandhi, examined the many kinds of economies found in nature[2] and concluded that in order to achieve even relative permanence, our human economy had to be some combination of nature's economies of '*service*' (i.e. selfless contribution), of '*gregation*' (contribution in return for communal rather than private benefits) and of '*enterprise*' (contribution in return for private benefits). Both Boulding and Kumarappa, early thinkers on 'sustainability', had in their own ways visioned economies of permanence which would meet human needs whilst recognizing limits and mimicking the regenerative cyclicality of natural systems.

The process of visioning an economy fit for our future received a boost over three decades later, when Walter Stahel and Genevieve Reday detailed their vision[3] of a closed-loop or circular economy, and its positive impact on job creation, economic competitiveness, resource savings, and waste prevention. Such work was based on holistic thinking about resource productivity, as against the conventional yardstick of labour productivity. A decade and a half later, von Weizsäcker and others presented further evidence of the possibility of significantly increasing resource productivity - by a factor of four.[4]

However, despite the increasing availability of relevant technology and economic justification for

Fig. 1 Healthy Economy, healthy humans, healthy planet?

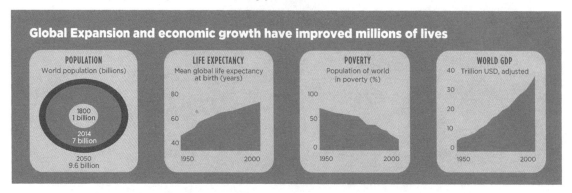

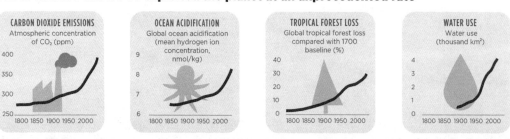

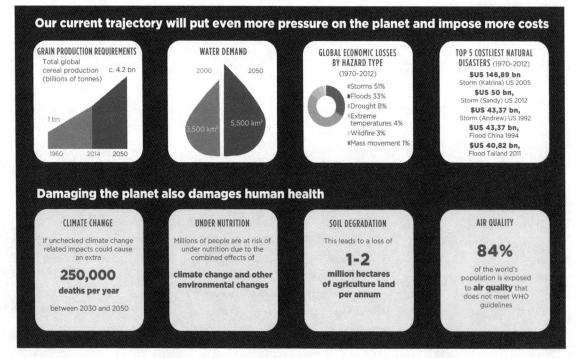

Source: Image adapted from a sharegraphic found on http://www.thelancet.com/infographics/planetary-health. Additional data from World Bank. 2015. The Little Green Data Book 2015. Washington, DC: World Bank. doi:10.1596/978-1-4648-0560-8 and UNEP (2015): UNEP Inquiry: The Coming Financial Climate – The Inquiry's 4th Progress Report

change, our dominant economic model remained a 'take-make-dispose' economy based on fuelling consumer demand, decreasing prices, increasing throughput, and ever-increasing ecological and environmental footprints. It created wealth in many countries for hundreds of millions, but left too many

1

UNCOVERING
PATHWAYS
TOWARDS AN
INCLUSIVE
GREEN ECONOMY

A SUMMARY FOR
LEADERS

❯ VISIONING
TOMORROW

in poverty and future generations exposed to risks and costs of the growing externalities of over-production and over-consumption.

Placing all humans and their well-being at the centre of an agenda for change, and sharply focussing on a few goals and quantifiable targets, the Millennium Development Goals (targeted for delivery this year, 2015) provided an anchor for policy change and socially responsible investment.

However, whilst addressing the needs of the bottom of the social and economic pyramid, these goals fell short of promoting development for all. That gap is now being filled by the Sustainable Development Goals (SDGs) to kick-start the 2030 Agenda for Sustainable Development. This Agenda and the SDGs offer an opportunity to reframe economic policy around the core elements of sustainability, lead very concretely by a focus on building and creating inclusive green economies.

Achieving the SDGs is central to the agenda being proposed here for an 'Inclusive Green Economy' through core elements comprising sustainable consumption and production, equitable outcomes, and investments for environmental sustainability. Focusing on the institutions, the rules of the game, and the policies and incentives that are shapers and drivers of markets, trade and finance will help achieve the SDGs by refocusing political attention and financial resources on better managing our common wealth and heritage.

In the pages that follow, we describe our key challenges in doing so as well as our proposed solutions to these challenges. We show how and why the Inclusive Green Economy provides for a "next stage" economic model to support sustainable development and the right incubator for the coming of Earth's spaceship economy, an Economy of Permanence.

1

UNCOVERING
PATHWAYS
TOWARDS AN
INCLUSIVE
GREEN ECONOMY

❯ VISIONING
TOMORROW

"Placing all humans and their well-being at the centre of an agenda for change." © ROBERTHARDING.COM

2

UNCOVERING
PATHWAYS
TOWARDS AN
INCLUSIVE
GREEN ECONOMY

A SUMMARY FOR
LEADERS

RECOGNIZING
TODAY

"The health impacts from environmental pollution and ecosystem degradation are borne to the largest extent by disadvantaged and vulnerable populations, including children and women". © SHUTTERSTOCK

Recognizing Today

2

UNCOVERING
PATHWAYS
TOWARDS AN
INCLUSIVE
GREEN ECONOMY

A SUMMARY FOR
LEADERS

⟩ RECOGNIZING
TODAY

The title of this section *"Chains of Challenge and the Challenges of Change"* is chosen purposefully. Firstly, departing from 'business as usual' is challenging predominantly because the changes we need are so universal and so interlinked that transition strategies can succeed only if addressed at a systemic, whole-economy, whole-society level. We enumerate some of these *"chains of challenge"* below to illustrate this point.

THE CHAINS OF CHALLENGE

It is increasingly the case that the most serious global problems of our time are anything but par-celled into convenient boxes; indeed, they form a vast meshwork of many chains, each linked to many others. Conventional thinking that positions development and environment as trade-offs, arguing that environmental quality can only *follow* after development needs are met has been challenged by the recognition of important realities discussed below but also by the emergence of a range of 'green' development strategies, practice, and technologies have evolved to enable the meeting of human needs whilst avoiding environmental destruction.

Human Health is harmed by environmental degradation and change:[5] Changing environments, such as climate, temperature, precipitation, can also pose new risks of communicable diseases. Newly recognized diseases, such as Ebola,[6] SARS,[7] and Avian flu[8] have been linked to environmental factors.

The health impacts from environmental pollution and ecosystem degradation are borne to the largest extent by disadvantaged and vulnerable populations, including children and women. Environment-related diseases not only impact the poor and vulnerable most heavily, but also contribute to perpetuating poverty. Environment-linked illnesses have a direct impact on economic productivity, at both the household and national levels, by reducing the ability to work.

Environmental damage from irresponsible practices in mining & industry comes with health costs & social unrest: Health risk from industry-induced contamination of land and water is one of the most common sources of local grievances, bearing the potential to ignite conflict. Social unrest over environmental contamination and inequitable outcomes of wealth from resource extraction has been observed in several countries.

Persistent poverty is exacerbated by ecosystem degradation: The bottom 40 per cent of the population shares less than 4 per cent of the global GDP. Most of these approximately 2 billion people live on small farms, around forests or coastlines, and are dependent on the productive capacity of nature and ecosystem services for their livelihoods and income-generating opportunities. Further degradation of natural resources and ecosystems will increase poverty, hunger, and economic inequality. The Economics of Ecosystems and Biodiversity (TEEB) estimated that ecosystem services and other non-marketed goods accounted for between

Fig 2: Food lost or wasted by region and stage in value chain, 2009 (percent of kcal lost or wasted)

2

UNCOVERING
PATHWAYS
TOWARDS AN
INCLUSIVE
GREEN ECONOMY

A SUMMARY FOR
LEADERS

⟩ RECOGNIZING
TODAY

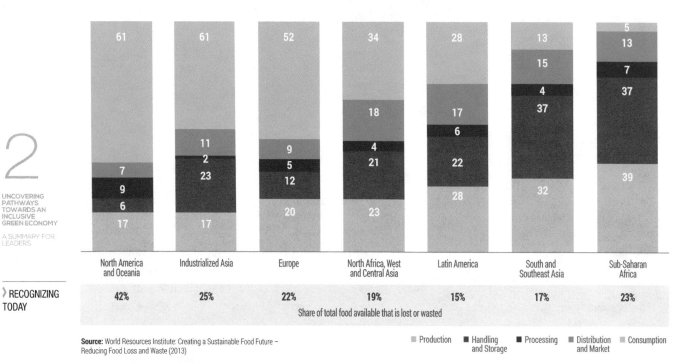

	North America and Oceania	Industrialized Asia	Europe	North Africa, West and Central Asia	Latin America	South and Southeast Asia	Sub-Saharan Africa
Consumption	61	61	52	34	28	13	5
Distribution and Market	11		9	18	17	15	13
Processing	7	2	5	4	6	4	7
Handling and Storage	9	23	12	21	22	37	37
Production	6						
	17	17	20	23	28	32	39
Share of total food available that is lost or wasted	**42%**	**25%**	**22%**	**19%**	**15%**	**17%**	**23%**

Source: World Resources Institute: Creating a Sustainable Food Future – Reducing Food Loss and Waste (2013)

- Production
- Handling and Storage
- Processing
- Distribution and Market
- Consumption

47 to 89 per cent of the "GDP of the poor" amongst large segments of the population in India, Indonesia and Brazil.[9]

Extreme Weather Events Destroy Jobs in Developed and Developing Countries: Although increasing frequency of extreme weather events across the world are widely recognized as part of the unfolding human tragedy of climate change, there is little public realization of their wider social cost in terms of lost jobs. Hurricane Katrina (2005) resulted in a loss of 40,000 jobs in the United States. And in addition to thousands of deaths, Cyclone Sidr (2007) in Bangladesh also affected thousands of small enterprises and led to over half a million job losses.[10]

The most vulnerable are worst affected by Climate Change: The most vulnerable people - low-income households, indigenous peoples, women and girls - bear a disproportionate share of the costs of environmental and ecological damage. Women's traditional responsibilities in developing countries as food growers, water and fuel gatherers, and caregivers connect them intimately to available natural resources and the climate, making them even more vulnerable to environmental hardships.[11]

A litany of problems are linked with fossil fuel subsidies: Fossil fuel subsidies have a negative impact on the environment, on the health of people, absorb substantial fiscal resources, often fail to benefit the targeted groups,

"The most vulnerable people bear a disproportionate share of the costs of environmental and ecological damage." © ROBERTHARDING.COM and encourage wasteful consumption of energy. They represent huge costs to society (including externalities) estimated by the IMF to exceed USD 2 trillion per year.[12]

Food - too little and too much: Food produced today embodies approximately 2,800 calories per person per day, or almost one third *more* than the amount needed to feed the world population.[13] Yet much of it is wasted. So it is perhaps the most humiliating failure of modern society and its dominant economic model that an estimated 805 million people in the world are still chronically undernourished, the vast majority (98 per cent) being in developing countries.[14] Conversely, almost two billion adults in the world are considered overweight, 600 million of whom are obese.[15]

Smallholder Farms, Food Security, Poverty, & Jobs: Smallholder farms (i.e. less than 2 hectares) represent over 475 million of the world's 570 million farms[16] and, in much of the developing world, they produce over 80 per cent of the food consumed.[17] Smallholder farming is by far the largest segment of jobs in agriculture: an estimated one billion. Sustainably improving yields and increasing incomes in the hands of these smallholders, whilst not destabilizing this form of farming as the largest source of employment is at once a food security challenge, an environmental challenge and humanity's foremost employment challenge.

'Eco-Agri-Food' systems and their externalities: Eighty per cent of new croplands are replacing tropical forests,[18] a pattern which is resulting in the loss of biodiversity and the loss or degradation of ecosystems including those essential for supporting agriculture. The economic environment in which farmers and agricultural policy-makers operate is distorted by significant externalities. Most of the largest impacts of various agricultural and food systems on the health of ecosystems, agricultural lands, waters, seas, and human beings are *economically invisible*, so they do not get the attention they deserve from governments or businesses. This is a root cause of fragility and low resilience in both ecological and human systems.

Ecological risks are Inter-related and global-local: Anthropogenic GHG emissions are driving not just *climate change*,[19] but also coral bleaching and *ocean acidification*, thus putting at risk coral reef biodiversity as well as the food, nutrition & livelihoods of an estimated 500 million coastal and island dwellers[20] dependent on fisheries and reef tourism. Rainforest dieback, part of the ecological boundary of *land system change* (another serious ecological risk), may happen as a result of *climate change*, and needs to be further evaluated as a serious threat to rainfall cycles and hence agricultural productivity.

CHALLENGES OF CHANGE

In her foreword to "Our Common Future", Gro Brundtland wrote[21] that the UN General Assembly's demand for a 'World Commission on Environment & Development' was *"a clear demonstration of the widespread feeling of frustration and inadequacy in the international community about our own ability to address the vital global issues and deal effectively with them."*

Almost three decades on, this sense of frustration highlighted by Dr. Brundtland has not diminished. The challenge of change is deep and many-dimensional. It includes addressing the drivers of inequalities, ecological scarcities, environmental risks, declining employment, misdirected finance, poor governance and an antiquated corporate agency – each representing a collection of major challenges and all having been recognized by the 2030 Agenda for Sustainable Development as significant barriers to the wellbeing of people, a healthy planet, prosperity, peace and global partnership.

The challenges below are all accentuated by *urgency* of transition that is needed towards an Inclusive Green Economy, in many cases are predicated by the pace at which we are heading towards ecological boundary constraints.[22] Socio-political tensions are equally worrying, ever more frequently boiling over into widespread violence and destruction, fuelled by a restive, dis-satisfied and largely internet-enabled population.

Fig 3: Everybody on the bus?

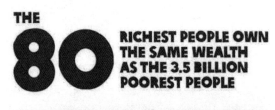

Source: Oxfam International.
https://www.oxfam.org/en/campaigns/even-it/take-action-fight-inequality-and-make-tax-fair

Inequalities

Inequalities remain unacceptably high across all dimensions of human life, and the resulting poverty may further aggravate environmental degradation. As for global wealth concentration, the richest 1 per cent of the world's population now control close to 50 per cent of global assets, while the poorest half owns just 1 per cent.[23] Meanwhile, the dominant economic model with 'free markets' as its centre stage has gained ground. It is true that markets serve many purposes well — such as price-discovery and efficient resource allocation — but it is also true that markets generally are not designed to solve social problems, in particular, the problem of inequitable outcomes. This points to the policy arena as a source of solutions.

Ecological Scarcities & Environmental Risks

Growing global and local ecological constraints are compounded by a combination of economic crises, natural disasters, and social conflict. Fresh water, fertile land, and clean air — the bedrock of natural wealth and human well-being - are increasingly scarce. In addition, global climate change may prove to be the biggest crisis humanity has ever faced, requiring us to rethink how we create prosperity, invest the proceeds, and create the conditions for a life of dignity for all in a finite world.

Declining Employment

Globalisation has brought with it immense progress and advancements but has also led to the loss of jobs in many sectors and geographical regions and increasing vulnerability of employment worldwide. Globally, 22 million manufacturing jobs were lost between 1995 and 2002, even as industrial output increased by 30 per cent.[24] The employment challenge is, therefore, a combination of the need for "more jobs", "better jobs" and "social inclusion".[25]

Misdirected Finance

Investment horizons, whether in terms of maturity of debts, scope of risk analysis or the focus of equity markets, are shorter than the lifetime of the assets and the impacts they create.[26] Owners of financial assets, including institutional investors representing hundreds of millions of pension and insurance policy holders, are drawing benefits from this stock of physical assets, making their owners dependent on their extended economic life and profitability.

These owners, and others with a stake in the fossil fuel economy, therefore, can and do apply their considerable political influence to slow down policy and other measures that might diminish, or

Fig 4: Sustainable finance: taking a systemic view.

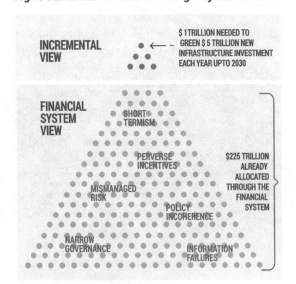

Source: UNEP Inquiry

2

UNCOVERING
PATHWAYS
TOWARDS AN
INCLUSIVE
GREEN ECONOMY

A SUMMARY FOR
LEADERS

› RECOGNIZING
TODAY

"strand", their assets` lifelong value. Although coal assets have in recent years diminished in value, the annual investment in fossil fuel exploitation continues to outpace investment in renewables by a factor of three.

Public finance can be an important driver and leader of private financial flows, but unfortunately, it is at present largely towards a 'brown economy'. Subsidies for fossil fuels (mentioned above) are a particularly egregious example of misdirected public finance, but financing for today's 'brown economy' is both large and sticky, and continues to be the majority of global 'Gross Capital Formation', representing an estimated annual 20 per cent of GDP worldwide.

Antiquated Corporate Social Contract

Looking more broadly, one sees a landscape of misaligned incentives and antiquated institutions guiding investment and economic activity. For example, delivering 60 per cent of GDP and providing 70 per cent of jobs, today's corporation is a truly influential institution, using marketing, advertising, and financial leverage to increase production and profits.[27] While contributing to an enhanced quality of life for many, if left unregulated, corporations are *arbitrageurs par excellence*: of natural resources (mining them from wherever they are cheapest and easiest to access); of labour (the more deregulated and cheaper, the better); of manufacturing capacity (especially subsidized capacity in countries that seek and underwrite industrialization); and of consumer markets (those with high concentrations of rich consumers willing to pay high prices for branded goods and services).

Recognizing the private sector as an engine for innovation, employment and economic growth, most governments have provided corporations with considerable support through licencing, concessions, tax and financing incentives, subsidies, and favourable trade tariffs. These factors have contributed to their success, and in turn corporations have added value and contributed to economic development and progress. However, corporations have also generated significant negative externalities in terms of environmental and social footprints. For example, the costs to society from "business as usual" (in the form of GHG emissions, pollution, freshwater scarcity, and conversion of natural areas, etc.) of the top three thousand listed corporations was estimated at $2.1 trillion,[28] or 3.5 per cent of global GDP. Modern society's social contract with the private sector, which accepts these public losses in the pursuit of private profits, is increasingly being called into question.

In summary...

Today's dominant economic model generates widespread and serious environmental and health risks; encourages a wasteful consumer and production culture; drives ecological and resource scarcities; and results in outcomes that create an unfair society. Addressing these problems calls for an economic system that speaks to the calls of the environment, social justice, and inclusiveness.

They call for a broader and more transformational and proactive role of public policy and the state to guide and enable more sustainable outcomes. The overarching challenge is of economic redesign: not incremental or piecemeal redesign, but one which is holistic and encompassing, transformational, and moves us towards an inclusive green economy that enables human well being.

Challenges to be addressed for inclusive green economy transformations and transitions are several: the pressure of time to make these transitions, the required knowledge, skills and technology, and the availability of information, finance and capacity to set the necessary changes in place. The social implications of transitions can be considerable and difficult to manage especially if they entail disruption of prevailing patterns of employment. In carbon-based economies, especially, issues will arise around stranded assets,[29] lost revenues and even stranded skills sets, as the economy reduces its dependency on fossil fuels. However, these very challenges define the work that lies ahead for politicians and leaders of businesses and civil society in a world increasingly troubled by concerns with environmental sustainability.

2

UNCOVERING
PATHWAYS
TOWARDS AN
INCLUSIVE
GREEN ECONOMY

A SUMMARY FOR
LEADERS

〉 RECOGNIZING
TODAY

**UNCOVERING
PATHWAYS
TOWARDS AN
INCLUSIVE
GREEN ECONOMY**

A SUMMARY FOR
LEADERS

› UNCOVERING
PATHWAYS
TOWARDS AN
INCLUSIVE GREEN
ECONOMY

"Incentivize and invest in an innovation-based inclusive green economy that will produce less, remanufacture more, reuse, recycle and restore; and set the stage for evolution towards a truly 'circular economy." © ROBERTHARDING.COM

Uncovering Pathways Towards an Inclusive Green Economy

3

UNCOVERING
PATHWAYS
TOWARDS AN
INCLUSIVE
GREEN ECONOMY

A SUMMARY FOR
LEADERS

〉 UNCOVERING
PATHWAYS
TOWARDS AN
INCLUSIVE GREEN
ECONOMY

Many approaches to sustainable development and well being have evolved over the last quarter century, reflecting different national contexts and priorities, sectoral concerns, and transitional strategies.[30] In 2008, UNEP proposed and anchored the 'green economy initiative' (GEI) of the United Nations in response to this evolution as well as the ongoing global financial crisis, out of the recognition that without a fundamental economic transformation, the goals of sustainable development would remain elusive.

A few years later in 2012, the *'Rio+20'* summit's outcome document "The Future We Want" recognised "green economy"[31] as an important tool for achieving sustainable development and poverty eradication. Since then, a large and growing number of countries have actively pursued green economy pathway, working with UN agencies and other stakeholders such as the Partnership for Action on Green Economy (PAGE), the Poverty-Environment Initiative (PEI), the Green Growth Knowledge Platform (GGKP) and the Global Green Growth Institute (GGGI) among others.

Today, 65 countries have embarked on green economy and related strategies, with 48 of them developing national green economy plans as the centerpiece of these strategies.[32] Despite this growing engagement with green initiatives, a number of major challenges still loom as discussed earlier, and even more transformational approaches are required.

DESIGN PRINCIPLES

An Inclusive Green Economy is based on sharing, circularity, collaboration, solidarity, resilience, opportunity, and interdependence. The design principles for an "Inclusive Green Economy" speak to these elements of a socio-ecological and economy-wide transition and call for economic and fiscal policy reforms, legislative changes, new technologies, changes in financing, and strong institutions that are specifically geared to safeguarding social and ecological floors. They include:

▶ **Centrality of Jobs and the Economy:** Seek economy-wide, cross-sectoral transformation by addressing all pillars of sustainability, hence "promoting sustained, inclusive and sustainable economic growth, full and productive employment and decent work for all";

▶ **Focus on Public Wealth:** Develop, maintain and invest in public wealth – i.e. physical and ecological infrastructure, constitutions, laws (eg: property rights & environmental legislation), and corporate governance standards

▶ **Investment in Ecological Infrastructure:** Amongst public assets, recognize the central role of healthy ecosystems to secure long-term well being and economic opportunity, & improved social outcomes. Recognize, measure, and respond to the economic significance of ecosystem services as a large fraction of the "GDP of the poor" in rural contexts in the developing world.

3

UNCOVERING
PATHWAYS
TOWARDS AN
INCLUSIVE
GREEN ECONOMY

A SUMMARY FOR
LEADERS

> UNCOVERING
PATHWAYS
TOWARDS AN
INCLUSIVE GREEN
ECONOMY

▸ **Operationalizing the Precautionary Principle:** Recognizing today's risks as tomorrow's costs to well being, legislate protective action or precaution even in the absence of complete scientific proof of major ecological risks and health risks arising from economic activity.

▸ **Innovation for Sustainability:** Recognize economic, social, environmental opportunities in all forms of innovation – social, institutional, financial & technological. Incentivize & invest in an innovation-based inclusive green economy that will produce with less, remanufacture more, reuse, recycle and restore; and set the stage for evolution towards a truly 'circular economy', an economy of permanence.

▸ **Natural Resource Conservation:** Promote resource efficiency, sustainable natural resource management, and sustainable consumption and production to address resource security concerns.

▸ **Human Resource Development:** Invest in human capabilities to enable people to determine outcomes and live their lives in dignity. Missing capabilities misalign the economy, environment, and society and lead to unsustainable development.

▸ **Building Institutions:** Invest in effective legislation and strong institutions for governance at local, regional and national levels, whilst ensuring transfers of knowledge and finance between these levels; ensure buy-in to green reform by providing clear fiscal stakes at different levels of government; encourage collaboration amongst ministries

▸ **Long-term versus Short-term:** Broadening the focus of policy reforms, incentives, subsidies, and market regulations from short-term stability to long-term resilience to address the real horizons of most sustainability challenges and to align financial markets and the real economy to serve the long-term interests of humanity.

▸ **'Micro-Policy' Reforms:** Private sector choices today largely determine resource use & economic direction, but regulations influence and incentives motivate firms to make choices. Identify & implement effective "micro-policy" reforms in key areas (such as corporate taxation, financial reporting, advertising standards, limits to leverage, etc) so that the private sector can be profitable whilst generating gains, not losses, in public wealth.

THE CENTRALITY OF JOBS

Work provides not merely the incomes we need for daily living, but meaning to our lives, social inclusion and self-respect. It is no surprise therefore that the largest concerns in any economy are around the very real risks of job losses and how to overcome them. Whilst social security and income support schemes can and do help, the only lasting solutions are new jobs, the so-named 'green and decent jobs' that the new economic model will generate. The good news is that new job opportunities in an inclusive green economy are significant, but they need to be identified early, and the education and skills training needed to fill them ought to be an early priority for any state engaging such a transition.

Renewable energy and waste management provide two such examples. Bringing electricity to unserved and underserved populations through the use of mini grid renewable energy systems is one of the most tangible contributions that an inclusive green economy can make to vulnerable communities, remote regions, and island states while also stimulating job creation and supporting social enterprise development. And in Brazil, China and the United States, the waste sector employs 12 million people, most of them extremely poor.[33]

The formalization of this sector via social policy measures and investments in green technology will ensure safer working conditions and open up opportunities to develop new skills and diversify future

Fig 5: The renewable energy sector created 6.5 million jobs in 2013

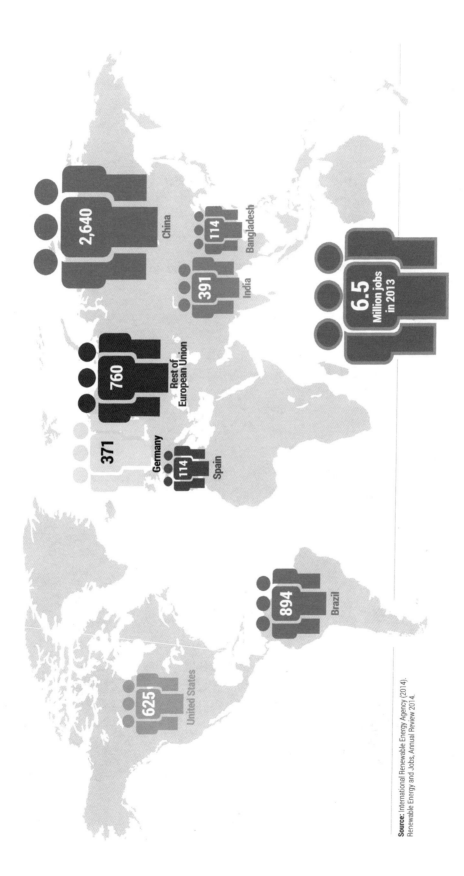

Source: International Renewable Energy Agency (2014).
Renewable Energy and Jobs, Annual Review 2014.

3

UNCOVERING
PATHWAYS
TOWARDS AN
INCLUSIVE
GREEN ECONOMY

A SUMMARY FOR
LEADERS

〉 UNCOVERING
PATHWAYS
TOWARDS AN
INCLUSIVE GREEN
ECONOMY

employment options. At the same time, recycling minimizes the need for raw-material extraction and has considerable energy savings.

Overall, the extent of the creation of 'green and decent jobs' in a country can be seen as an indicator of competitiveness: the higher it is, the better poised the country is to compete in a foreseeable future in which economies are designed to produce wealth and income without creating environmental risks and ecological scarcities.

EMBRACING A CIRCULAR AND A SHARING ECONOMY

The shift to sustainable patterns of consumption and production (SCP) is central to balancing human activities with the long-term functioning of ecosystems. By embedding SCP systems in national governance and sectoral policies, rethinking unbridled consumerism, and balancing over and under consumption can enable the unserved and underserved to access key supply constrained resources while maintaining a harmony with earth's life support system.

A range of innovation and enterprise can be triggered by applying principles of a 'circular economy', an economy that is regenerative and designed *ab initio* to eradicate waste and return nutrients and water to ecosystems. It departs radically from our dominant "take, make, waste" linear model of production and consumption. It is based on whole-systems thinking and inspired by the living natural world in which 'waste' from one species becomes 'food' for another, and so on in cyclical systemic self-sufficiency. From its very origins in the early work of Walter Stahel[34] and others, the concept of the 'circular economy' has been rooted in the pursuit of higher employment, and in the idea that business should be selling utilization rather than selling goods, thus enabling closer monitoring and control over end-of-life disposal versus re-deployment of biotic and abiotic materials.

"A range of innovation and enterprise can be triggered by applying principles of a 'circular economy', an economy that is regenerative and designed ab initio to eradicate waste and return nutrients and water to ecosystems." © ROBERTHARDING.COM

Fig. 6 - Decoupling the link between resource use and economic growth requires innovative solutions.

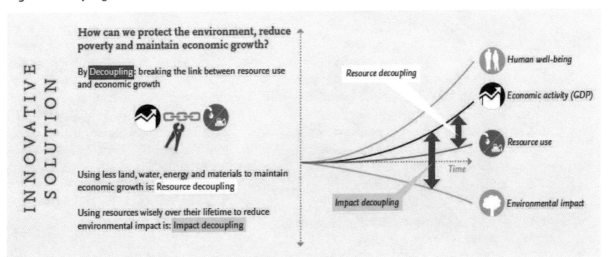

Source: Secretariat of the International Resource Panel

Fig 7: Envisioning an economy that is circular and green

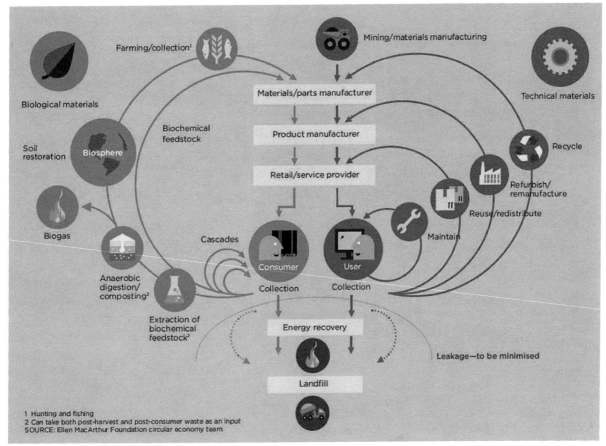

Source: Ellen MacArthur Foundation (2013). Towards the Circular Economy: Opportunities for the consumer goods sector.

3

UNCOVERING
PATHWAYS
TOWARDS AN
INCLUSIVE
GREEN ECONOMY

A SUMMARY FOR
LEADERS

⟩ UNCOVERING
PATHWAYS
TOWARDS AN
INCLUSIVE GREEN
ECONOMY

3

UNCOVERING
PATHWAYS
TOWARDS AN
INCLUSIVE
GREEN ECONOMY

A SUMMARY FOR
LEADERS

> UNCOVERING
PATHWAYS
TOWARDS AN
INCLUSIVE GREEN
ECONOMY

Numerous movements, initiatives and projects have spontaneously emerged to advance more sustainable ways of living. Their potential for achieving resource efficiency, reducing environmental impacts, creating jobs and improving well-being is increasingly recognized. New ICTs, such as mobile applications and geographic information systems, as well as the growing virtual communities are amongst the technological developments that strongly support and enable the emergence and development of sharing practices. The "sharing" economy, the move to more common resource use, refers to the broad range of product-service systems, sharing and swapping practices that decouple ownership of a good from its use, while re-installing social interactions and trust within a community of people having similar interests. Examples include lodging, transportation, home Wi-Fi network or power-tools sharing, clothes swapping, bicycles, carpooling etc.[35] Sharing practices and models are typically less resource intensive, as fewer products are produced to provide the same service to more people. They also open the door to a new sense of well-being and comfort, as product maintenance, services and disposal are typically not the responsibility of the individual user.

Sharing practices have existed for a long time amongst communities, neighbours, families, friends; in some cases, they are directly inspired by traditional social practices. These practices are now globalized into profitable business models that contribute to shaping a new, more sustainable, and well-being oriented economy. However, these emerging models remain mostly local, and are seldom scaled up or transferred to other contexts. This is often due to the fact that these innovative models lack the appropriate regulatory frameworks, investments and economic incentives that would allow them to grow and expand.[36]

ECOLOGICAL VALUE, THE PRECAUTIONARY PRINCIPLE, AND CRITICAL NATURAL CAPITAL

Reflecting on the importance of nature and the environment to human well-being will help to balance and restore its rightful place in sustainable development. There are many worldviews of the human-nature inter-relationship and concepts that emerge from these worldviews, but which have universal resonances. In the Andean cultures the concept of 'Sumak Kawsay' or "living well" sees the individual within his or her social and cultural communities and in relation to their natural environment pursuing harmonious collective development (See figure 7). In addition, the "Rights of Nature" perspective[37] - promoted by ecologists like Aldo Leopold - reflects the view that nature has an intrinsic value that is independent of its human, instrumental relevance and which need to be recognized.[38] China`s vision of an "ecological civilization" is another example of stewardship. Gandhi's concept of 'trusteeship' speaks to the idea that we are trustees of the earth's endowments and, thus, that we must see ourselves not as their 'owners', but as 'trustees', who manage them today for all peoples and for future generations.

Through the 2030 Agenda for Sustainable Development, Member States have reaffirmed that "planet Earth and its ecosystems are our common home and that 'Mother Earth' is a common expression in a number of countries and regions."

A failure to recognize serious ecological constraints is a failure to acknowledge the needs and rights of future generations—or in some cases for current generations. Once a floor or a ceiling is reached, the rules of the game change and survival itself may become a challenge, regardless of the offsetting stock of financial or human capital. The understanding of what constitutes 'critical natural capital' is changing rapidly as we approach ecological boundaries and binding constraints owing to cumulative impacts.[39] The ozone layer has been cited as an example of critical natural capital – there is no known technology-based substitute and its functionality is critical to human wellbeing.

A comprehensive accounting of natural wealth and degradation is therefore key to internalize the "invisibility of nature" in overall economic performance. Valuing ecosystem services that both

Fig 8: Multiple approaches towards environmental sustainability - Bolivia's concept of Living Well in and Harmony and Balance with Mother Earth

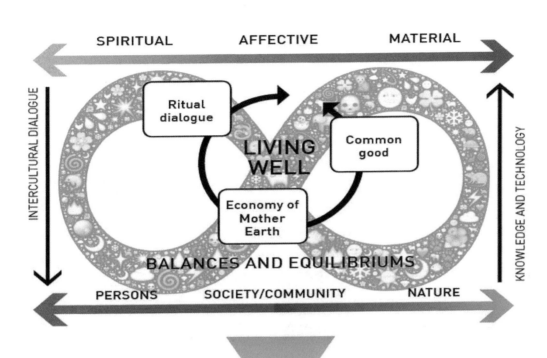

Source: UNEP (2015). Multiple Pathways to Sustainable Development: initial findings from the global south, p. 33

3

UNCOVERING
PATHWAYS
TOWARDS AN
INCLUSIVE
GREEN ECONOMY

A SUMMARY FOR
LEADERS

UNCOVERING
PATHWAYS
TOWARDS AN
INCLUSIVE GREEN
ECONOMY

provide goods and regulate ecosystem processes of benefit to people such as climate and water, serve as important aids to decision making with regard to prioritising ecosystem sustainability.

The purpose of valuing ecosystem services is not to privatize them or make them into commodities for the market. Instead, valuing can be a crucial management tool to understand and act to conserve ecosystems and reduce the development pressure on them. Fundamentally, accounting for natural capital and degradation in a nation's economic performance enables a better understanding of the direction and sustainability of long term well being of its people.

Fig 9: Growing wealth

Percentage change in wealth 1990 - 2010 (per capita)

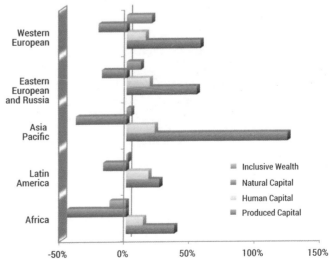

Source: Inclusive Wealth Index

❯ UNCOVERING
PATHWAYS
TOWARDS AN
INCLUSIVE GREEN
ECONOMY

KEY POLICY CHOICES FOR TRANSFORMATIVE CHANGE

The space of policy solutions towards an inclusive green economy is wide, and needs to be cultivated and considered simultaneously in order to be effective as a template for economic transition. Some key policy choices are listed below towards investing for environmental sustainability, promoting SCP systems, and pursuing inclusive outcomes.

INVESTMENTS FOR ENVIRONMENTAL SUSTAINABILITY

▸ Support action towards a **better alignment of rules that govern financial markets** with long term sustainable development[40]

▸ **Reallocate capital toward green investments**, the greening of manufacturing and other economic sectors to build more climate resilient- and sustainable communities and nations.

▸ **Build political and social consensus** towards transitions in carbon-based economies;

▸ **Invest in skills and capacity** for increased competitiveness, innovation, and positioning within a globalized green economy.

▸ **Adopt industrial ecological practices** so as to enhance resource security, reduce environmental pressure, promote competitiveness and increase revenues.

▸ **Create new sustainable business opportunities and green and decent jobs** through investments in renewable energy, green infrastructure such as sustainable buildings, effective and efficient public transportation, sustainable agriculture, and sustainable natural resource management.

▸ Invest in: (a) **science, R & D, big data** to address environmental challenges; (b) Information and Communications Technologies (ICT) to inform, share, scale up and deliver; (c) build resilient smart cities using ICT to maximize integration of renewable energy in buildings, transport and local grids.

▸ Invest in **ecosystem restoration** and rebuilding of natural capital

PROMOTING SUSTAINABLE PRODUCTION CONSUMPTON SYSTEMS

▸ Move towards a **circular economy**: Recover, recycle, reuse, and remanufacture

▸ Mainstream **resource efficiency** in the economy through a focus on systems and practice – food and energy provisioning, mobility, housing, etc.

▸ **Reduce waste.** Where waste is produced, regard it as a resource, an investment and an employment opportunity.

▸ Invest in **eco-innovation** and cleaner manufacturing practices.

▸ **Internalize environmental and social externalities**, in order to provide the right market signals. Support the valuation of natural capital in economic decision-making and as a management tool, counteracting the persistence of negative externalities to the detriment of public value.

▸ Adopt the **valuation of natural capital in national accounts** and development indexes, as it enables a country to develop a sense of

"Towards a circular economy: Recover, recycle, reuse, and remanufacture." © ROBERTHARDING.COM

"Adopt the valuation of natural capital in national accounts." © ROBERTHARDING.COM

3

UNCOVERING
PATHWAYS
TOWARDS AN
INCLUSIVE
GREEN ECONOMY

A SUMMARY FOR
LEADERS

❯ UNCOVERING
PATHWAYS
TOWARDS AN
INCLUSIVE GREEN
ECONOMY

its "true wealth"; and value the natural capital degraded or used up in economic processes, as it provides a measure of "true income".

▸ Adopt policy mixes with **appropriate regulatory, behavioural, information-based and economic instruments** for addressing sustainable production and consumption challenges in priority areas such as water use, energy use, chemicals use and waste management.

▸ Revise the normative frameworks to include the necessary incentives and regulations that will provide the enabling conditions to adopt **sustainable and low carbon lifestyles**.

▸ Encourage an **inclusive sharing economy** to improve the efficiency and sustainability of resource use.

▸ **Invest in education and social interactions and hubs**, to change mind-sets and social practices and incorporate the concept of en-

vironmental sustainability in daily life and social practice, raise awareness of sustainable lifestyles, and facilitate change in consumer culture.

▸ Regard **youth as central to the goal of building a new global discourse** and solutions for IGE i.e., as ambassadors, as users of social media, and as future entrepreneurs and decision-makers.

▸ **Partner with both mainstream and social media** to build the elements of the public discourse.

▸ Implement existing policies to **address health issues** related to chemical and hazardous substances and indoor/outdoor air pollution, while addressing the knowledge, financing and technology gaps

▸ Develop consumer informational tools such as **labelling and certification**, which encourage behavioral change and green trade.

3

UNCOVERING
PATHWAYS
TOWARDS AN
INCLUSIVE
GREEN ECONOMY

A SUMMARY FOR
LEADERS

> UNCOVERING
PATHWAYS
TOWARDS AN
INCLUSIVE GREEN
ECONOMY

PURSUING INCLUSIVE OUTCOMES

▸ Protect the environment for **intra- and inter-generational equity and well-being**, and for the rights of nature,

▸ Recognize that **wellbeing of nature cannot be left to market forces**, but must be instead formed by choices we make as societies, nations and economies

▸ Enact fiscal policy reforms **that shift tax burdens away from labour and income and towards environmental and social externalities** and rents from scarce resources, to incentivize resource efficiencies and to reduce inequalities.

▸ **Eliminate fossil fuel subsidies with social strategies** to ensure that the poor are not adversely affected, and by building political consensus and understanding of their harmful effects.

▸ Address social implications of transitional issues head on by **creating social floors**, which guarantee basic protections to health care and income security.

▸ **Anticipate the losses** that may accompany the transition from an economy based on non-renewables to a more diversified mix, including from renewable resources, and minimize these through reskilling, intensified training, promotion of job placement in renewable jobs, and social safety nets.

▸ Support the creation of institutions and mechanisms for **equitable access to- and sharing of benefits** from natural resource development at the local and national levels.

"Revise the normative frameworks to include the necessary incentives and regulations that will provide the enabling conditions to adopt sustainable and low carbon lifestyles." © ROBERTHARDING.COM

"Invest in education and social interactions and hubs, to change mind-sets and social practices." © ROBERTHARDING.COM

3

UNCOVERING
PATHWAYS
TOWARDS AN
INCLUSIVE
GREEN ECONOMY

A SUMMARY FOR
LEADERS

> UNCOVERING
PATHWAYS
TOWARDS AN
INCLUSIVE GREEN
ECONOMY

▸ **Introduce a carbon price** and recycle the proceeds to support climate adaptation and mitigation.

▸ Invest in more labour intensive sources of growth such as agriculture, **horticulture, creative industry**, and also in the "productive assets of the poor".

> COLLABORATORS
AND CHAMPIONS

"Collaboration and championship are essential drivers of the changes we seek for replicating successes and scaling up an inclusive green economy." © ROBERTHARDING.COM

Collaborators and Champions

Citizens, Communities, Businesses, Finance, Governments

4

UNCOVERING
PATHWAYS
TOWARDS AN
INCLUSIVE
GREEN ECONOMY

A SUMMARY FOR
LEADERS

⟩ COLLABORATORS
AND CHAMPIONS

Given the complexity of our numerous 'chains of challenge' and the enormous size of our 'challenge of change', it is evident that nothing short of global cooperation and collaboration is needed across all tiers of decision-makers in society: governments, communities, businesses and citizens. Overwhelming societal challenges have been faced and overcome before in human history through such consensus and concerted action, but usually in times of war and natural calamity. In fewer instances, we have also succeeded in solving enormous environmental problems, at a regional level (eg: acid rain) and even at a global level (eg: ozone depletion).

The Montreal Protocol and subsequent actions to phase out ozone depleting substances will have prevented 2 million cases of skin cancer annually by 2030 while contributing to international goals to reduce emission of greenhouse gases.[41] The 2030 Agenda for Sustainable Development provides a historic opportunity to achieve unprecedented global cooperation and transformation. But how can we replicate such successes, and scale them up?

REPLICATING AND SCALING SUCCESSES

In many situations, scaling up innovations requires not just technological advancement, but also financial, institutional, and social changes. There is ample evidence of the power of finance and institutions to drive change, where technological innovations are being adopted and scaled up as a result of policy innovations, as for example providing renewable energy options to unserved populations.

Collaboration and championship are essential drivers of the changes we seek for replicating successes and scaling up an inclusive green economy. It is not widely understood how multi-tiered such collaboration needs to be, nor how important an element it has been in delivering the success we seek. Integrated approaches are needed that bring together all important stakeholders – businesses, financiers, technical communities, policy-makers, and technology users – to tackle barriers at multiple levels that hinder ability to attract, access, and absorb environmentally sound technology.

The Montreal Protocol has been hailed for its success in the transfer to developing countries of ozone-friendly technologies, but a large part of its success was related to the investment of the multilateral fund in capacity-building and regional and national actions to help transitions at many levels.

Secondly, the power of example needs to be used much more than it has been so far. Across countries, communities, sectors, and businesses, there are many success stories of policies, economic mechanisms, practices, and business models that demonstrate alternative ways forward. These stories need to be told, and retold.

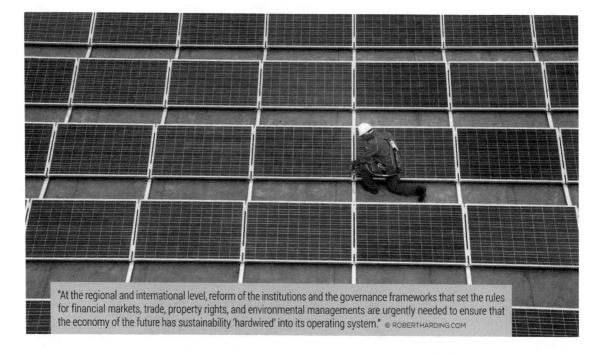

"At the regional and international level, reform of the institutions and the governance frameworks that set the rules for financial markets, trade, property rights, and environmental managements are urgently needed to ensure that the economy of the future has sustainability 'hardwired' into its operating system." © ROBERTHARDING.COM

4

UNCOVERING
PATHWAYS
TOWARDS AN
INCLUSIVE
GREEN ECONOMY

A SUMMARY FOR
LEADERS

❯ COLLABORATORS
AND CHAMPIONS

COLLABORATION ACROSS TIERS OF DECISION-MAKERS

Achieving transition to sustainable development through anan Inclusive Green Economy is a responsibility shared by governments, businesses, communities and citizens because all these decision-makers can through their actions either exacerbate or help to solve our meshwork of problems. Through the 2030 Agenda for Sustainable Development, Member States have said they are "determined to mobilize the means required to implement this Agenda through a revitalised Global Partnership for Sustainable Development, based on a spirit of strengthened global solidarity, focused in particular on the needs of the poorest and most vulnerable and with the participation of all countries, all stakeholders and all people." We enumerate some of the key areas and levels where such collaboration will need to focus.

At the regional and international level, reform of the institutions and the governance frameworks that set the rules for financial markets, trade, property rights, and environmental management are urgently needed to ensure that the economy

of the future has sustainability "hardwired" into its operating system. On trade, WTO has recognized the relationship between trade and sustainable development but further efforts are needed to make the WTO rules coherent with multilateral environmental agreements (trade-environment-related aspects) in order to preserve biodiversity, protect human health and prevent pollution and illegal trade of environmental resources.

Additionally, international norms and governance structures on technology transfer will be crucial building blocks of a sustainable economy. International and regional institutions and governance structures for environmental safeguards and decent jobs will also be also vital for ensuring IGE transition at the global and regional levels.

The task of corporate redesign – transforming business for tomorrow's world[42] - includes challenges such as reporting externalities; making advertising accountable; limiting corporate leverage; and reducing indiscriminate lobbying. The task of recognizing, measuring, valuing and reporting externalities so that a company's impacts and "True Economic Value Added" (TRU-EVA)[43] can be observed and responded to by business management, industry regulators, and society at large needs the collaboration and leadership of national and international accountancy regulators. Promoting accountable advertising - to inform rather than merely persuade the consumer - will need to be driven both by corporate champions and advertising associations, and encouraged by trade associations and national governments.

The unique position of local governments and capabilities of private sector leaders to leverage communities and to solve problems is very important for an inclusive green economy to take hold and scale in developing countries. Low-cost housing, clean energy, safe drinking water, sanitation, and other basic services can be provided by small and medium sized enterprises (SMEs) through cost-effective, low-carbon, ecologically friendly, and low maintenance technologies. SMEs are important drivers of growth in low-income economies and account for up to 90 per cent of all businesses across Sub Saharan Africa.[44]

Collaboration and championship are essential in the realm of finance for an inclusive green economy. As pointed out in UNEP's *Inquiry*,[45] changes are needed both on the *demand side* of finance – through pricing

reforms, smart public finance and environmental regulation to improve the risk: return ratio for green investments, and also on the *supply side* of finance - to address market failings such as short-termism, inadequate information, misaligned incentives, inadequate risk management, and incumbents' resistance to positive changes. To achieve this will need collaboration across central banks and regulators of banking, insurance and investment sectors, stock exchanges, and the Socially Responsible Investment (SRI) and Environmental, Social and Governance (ESG) and Impact Investing sectors as UNEP's work with finance institutions shows. Recognising that the establishment of an enabling environment for sustainable finance will take time, and cogniscent of the urgency of the sustainability agenda, the UNEP Finance Initiative is seeking to promote a market-driven, impact-based response to the fulfilment of the Sustainable Development Goals (SDGs - see figure 9), led by a combination of corporates, banks and investors. In addition, there is need to scale up innovations in insurance and to build risk capacity of nations.[46] Ultimately, financing the sustainability transition will require new skills and behaviours among the millions of professionals who work in the financial sector as well as in financial policy institutions and regulators. This means new initiatives to create

4

UNCOVERING
PATHWAYS
TOWARDS AN
INCLUSIVE
GREEN ECONOMY

A SUMMARY FOR
LEADERS

〉 COLLABORATORS
AND CHAMPIONS

"Empowerment will be driven through recognizing and protecting the different sets of rights and privileges that underpin a democratic society." © ROBERTHARDING.COM

financial cultures that incorporate the sustainability imperative into institutional values, incentives and core competencies – in essence, building the 'fit and proper' financial system for the 21st century green economy.

Finally, the engagement of civil society and consumers through institutions, open platforms, and governance frameworks needs to be ensured. Empowerment will be driven through recognizing and protecting the different sets of rights and privileges that underpin a democratic society, including: property rights; business rights; employment rights; public participation, access to justice and the rule of law. In this regard, information disclosure (including project plans and environmental assessments, the state of the environment, etc.), e-government, and public hearings for major environmental decision-making are essential mechanisms of transparent and collaborative governance.

TELLING AND RE-TELLING SUCCESS STORIES

It is good news that despite the predominance of unsustainable "business as usual" around the world, there are numerous stories emerging of the success of alternative approaches to development. These success stories need to be told and retold.

"Nature is not merely a luxury for the rich, it is a necessity for the poor and a vital part of human well-being for all." © ROBERTHARDING.COM

As we have noted earlier,[47] nature is not merely a luxury for the rich, it is a necessity for the poor and a vital part of human well-being for all. Destroying the natural commons, especially in rural areas in the developing world, is tantamount to destroying a large part of the 'GDP of the poor'. Furthermore, it is not the case that all developed nations are environmental graveyards, nor that natural-resource-starved nations cannot afford green development. Japan, a highly developed nation with limited natural resources boasts some of the highest recycling rates in the world. Singapore has created and sustained an economy of services which is highly decoupled from resource consumption. Barbados, a developing nation with limited resources, adopted a national green economy strategy well before Rio+20 put the term into common parlance across countries.

These countries were and are, in their own ways and contexts, champions of a new and inclusive green economy. We can all learn from these resource-constrained developed and developing countries because they recognized early on that resource efficiency, self-reliance and innovation are the drivers of improved human well-being in the absence of endless frontiers or unlimited stocks of natural resources. These efforts will ease their pathways towards achieving the SDGs and the 2030 Agenda for Sustainable Development.

However, the power of positive stories and the inspiration of champions can only be felt if such stories get told and retold across the world. And whilst emerging social media may provide some channels for such communication, they need to be reinforced through a concerted and collaborative effort by governments, media and advertising agencies, and billions of concerned and aware citizens around the world.

Fig 10: The Sustainable Development Goals

Source: www.globalgoals.org (accessed September 21, 2015)

4

UNCOVERING
PATHWAYS
TOWARDS AN
INCLUSIVE
GREEN ECONOMY

A SUMMARY FOR
LEADERS

⟩ COLLABORATORS
AND CHAMPIONS

UNCOVERING
PATHWAYS
TOWARDS AN
INCLUSIVE
GREEN ECONOMY

A SUMMARY FOR
LEADERS

> **ENDNOTES**

"An Inclusive Green Economy is based on sharing, circularity, collaboration, solidarity, resilience, opportunity, and interdependence." © ROBERTHARDING.COM

Endnotes

1   Kenneth E. Boulding. (1966), *"The Economics of the Coming Spaceship Earth"*, In H. Jarrett (ed.), Environmental Quality in a Growing Economy, Baltimore, MD: Johns Hopkins University Press, pp. 3-14

2   J.C. Kumarappa, (1945), *"Economy of Permanence"*, Sarva Seva Sangh Prakashan, Rajghat

3   W. Stahel & G. Reday, (1981), *"Jobs for Tomorrow, the potential for substituting manpower for energy"* by Vantage Press, New York, N.Y.

4   Ernst von Weizsäcker; Amory B. Lovins; L.Hunter Lovins, (1998), *"Factor Four: Doubling Wealth, Halving Resource Use"*, Earthscan

5   See WHO. 2008. Global Burden of Disease 2004 update available at *http://www.who.int/topics/global_burden_of_disease/en/*; CBD and WHO 2015. Connecting Global priorities: Biodiversity and Human Health available at *https://www.cbd.int/health/SOK-biodiversity-en.pdf*); S Whitmee, A Haines, et al. (2015) Safeguarding Human Health in the Anthropocene Epoch: Report of The Rockefeller Foundation–Lancet Commission on Planetary Health available at *http://www.thelancet.com/pdfs/journals/lancet/PIIS0140-6736(15)60901-1.pdf*;

6   S Ng et al, (2014). *"Association between temperature, humidity and ebolavirus disease outbreaks in Africa, 1976 to 2014"*; available at www.eurosurveillance.org/images/dynamic/EE/V19N35/art20892.pdf

7   Tan et al. (2005) *"An initial investigation of the association between the SARS outbreak and weather: with the view of the environmental temperature and its variation"*, J Epidemiol Community Health ;59:186-192, available at *www.jech.bmj.com/content/59/3/186.full*

8   Si, Y., T. Wang, A. K. Skidmore, W. F. De Boer, L. Li, and H. H. T. Prins. (2010). *"Environmental factors influencing the spread of the highly pathogenic avian influenza H5N1 virus in wild birds in Europe"*. Ecology and Society 15(3): 26. www.ecologyandsociety.org/vol15/iss3/art26/

9   10 TEEB (2010), *"The Economics of Ecosystems and Biodiversity: Mainstreaming the Economics of Nature: A Synthesis of the Approach, Conclusions and Recommendations of TEEB"*

10 ILO, (2013). *"Sustainable Development: Decent work and green jobs"*. Geneva

11 *www.undp.org/content/undp/en/home/librarypage/results/fast_facts/ff-gender-environment/*

12 *"Fossil Fuel Subsidies Costing Global Economy $2 Trillion: IMF."* Renew Economy. N.p., 28 Apr. 2014. Web. 20 Mar. 2015. *www.reneweconomy.com.au/2014/fossil-fuel-subsidies-costing-global-economy-2-trillion-imf-79534*

13 *"Food security indicators"*, FAO, (2014)

14 FAO, IFAD and WFP (2014), *"The State of Food Insecurity in the World 2014 - Strengthening the enabling environment for food security and nutrition"*. Rome, FAO.

15 *www.who.int/mediacentre/factsheets/fs311/en/*

16 FAO State of Food and Agriculture (2014)

17 *www.ifad.org/media/press/2013/27.htm*

18 Foley, J.A. et al. (2011) *"Solutions for a cultivated landscape,"* Nature, 478: 337-342.

19 Steffen et al. (2015), *"Planetary Boundaries: Guiding Human Development on a Changing Planet"*, Science Vol. 347 no. 6223 DOI: 10.1126/science.1259855

20 Wilkinson, C.r. (ed.) (2004) *"Status of the coral reefs of the world"*. Volumes 1 and 2. Australian institute for Marine Sciences, Townsville, Australia.

21 UN, (1987), *"Report of the World Commission on Environment and Development: Our Common Future"*

22 Steffen et al(2015), *"Planetary Boundaries: Guiding Human Development on a Changing Planet"*, Science Vol. 347 no. 6223 DOI: 10.1126/science.1259855

23 United Nations World Institute for Development Economics Research of the United Nations University (2006). *"The World Distribution of Household Wealth"*. NB: According to Credit Suisse 2014. Global Wealth Report 2014, the share has increased to almost 50%. See also the Oxfam report at *www.oxfamamerica.org/static/media/files/even-it-up-inequality-oxfam.pdf*

24 McAfee, A. (2013). *"Manufacturing Jobs and the Rise of the Machines"*. Harvard Business Review [online]. January 29th 2013.

25   ILO, 2013. Sustainable Development, Decent work and Green Jobs. Report V. Geneva

26   Inquiry: Design of a Sustainable Financial System. Report 3. (2015). p. 5

27   P Sukhdev (2012) *"Corporation 2020"*, Island Press, Washington DC

28   Trucost, (2010), for UN-PRI (Ed. UNEP-FI & UN Global Compact), Universal Owner Project, Report on Universal Ownership and Environmental Externalities

29   C McGlade and P Ekins (2015) paper shows that a third of fossil fuels will become stranded if international climate policy were to hold to the 2 degree limit. In *"The geographical distribution of fossil fuels unused when limiting global warming to 2ºC"*. Nature. Volume 157

30   For details see *www.unep.org/greeneconomy/portals/88/ repository/UNEP-SSC-China.pdf* The need for pluralistic approaches to addressing environmental sustainability has also been articulated at several levels, and reflected in UNEP Governing Council decisions (GC 27/8); Accessible at *www. unep.org/gc/gc27/docs/Decisions_adopted_by_the_first_ universal_session_%28advance%29.pdf*; more recently, under UNEA Resolution 1/10 on Different visions, approaches, models and tools to achieve environmental sustainability in the context of sustainable development and poverty eradication, SAMOA Pathways, the outcome document of the 3rd International Conference on Small Island Developing States (SIDS) in its paragraph 25, accessible at *www.sids2014.org/index. php?menu=1537*; Also see Agenda 21, JPOI, Rio +20, Millennium Declaration.

31   UNEP hosted and many other United Nations agencies participated in the *"Green Economy Initiative"*, one of nine 'Joint Crisis Initiatives' launched by the UN Secretary General in 2009 in response to the Global Financial Crisis. They evolved and agreed this definition of the *"green economy"*. There had been many earlier definitions of *"green economy"*, the earliest of which was in Pearce, Barbier & Markandya, "Blueprint for a Green Economy", 1989, Earthscan

32   For an update on such initiatives, see *www.unep.org/ greeneconomy/Portals/88/documents/GEI%20Highlights/GE_ flyer_October27_web-ready.pdf*

33   UNEP (2013). Green Economy Report – *"Waste: Investing in energy and resource efficiency"*, pg. 291. *www.unep.org/ greeneconomy/Portals/88/documents/ger/GER_8_Waste.pdf*

34   *"Jobs for Tomorrow: The Potential for Substituting Manpower for Energy , (1982),* and *"The Product-Life Factor"*, (1981)

35   see for example airbnb; *www.reuters.com/article/2014/03/20/ us-airbnb-financing-idUSBREA2J17Z20140320*;

36   see The Economist April 26, 2014; and the Harvard Business Review, October 13, 2014 at *www.hbr.org/2014/10/how- uber-and-the-sharing-economy-can-win-over-regulators/* for a discussion on this issue

37   See *www.pachamama.org/advocacy/rights-of-nature*; *www. therightsofnature.org/what-is-rights-of-nature/*

38   For a discussion on intrinsic and instrumental value of nature, see *www.nature.com/scitable/knowledge/library/intrinsic-value- ecology-and-conservation-25815400*

39   Rockstrom et al. (2009). *"Planetary Boundaries: Exploring the safe operating space for humanity"*. Ecology and Society 14(2): 32

40   For the publications of UNEP Inquiry, see *http://web.unep.org/ inquiry/publications*

41   Scientific Assessment of Ozone Depletion 2014. UNEP and WMO

42   P Sukhdev 2012 *"Corporation 2020"*, Island Press

43   Repetto, Robert, and Daniel Dias. (2006) *"TRUEVA: A New Integrated Financial Measure of Environmental Exposure."* In Yale Center for Environmental Law & Policy Working Paper Series, edited by Anastasia O'Rourke

44   IFC (2013). IFC Jobs Study: *"Assessing private sector contributions to job creation and poverty reduction"*, p. 4. *www.ifc.org/wps/wcm/connect/0fe6e2804e2c0a8f8d3bad7a9 dd66321/IFC_FULL+JOB+STUDY+REPORT_JAN2013_FINAL. pdf?MOD=AJPERES*

45   *"Inquiry into the Design of a Sustainable Financial System: Policy Innovations for a Green Economy"*, UNEP, (2015), available at *www.unep.org/greeneconomy/financialinquiry/portals/50215/ Inquiry_expanded.pdf*; see also *apps.unep.org/publications/index. php?option=com_pub&task=download&file=011401_en*

46   For some of the UNEP FI publications, see *www.unepfi. org/publications/*. More recent publications on sustainable insurance are available at *www.unepfi.org/publications/ insurance/*

47   *"The Economics of Ecosystems & Biodiversity – Interim Report"*, European Communities, (2008)

UNCOVERING
PATHWAYS
TOWARDS AN
INCLUSIVE
GREEN ECONOMY

A SUMMARY FOR
LEADERS

❭ ENDNOTES